Drawing Shapes

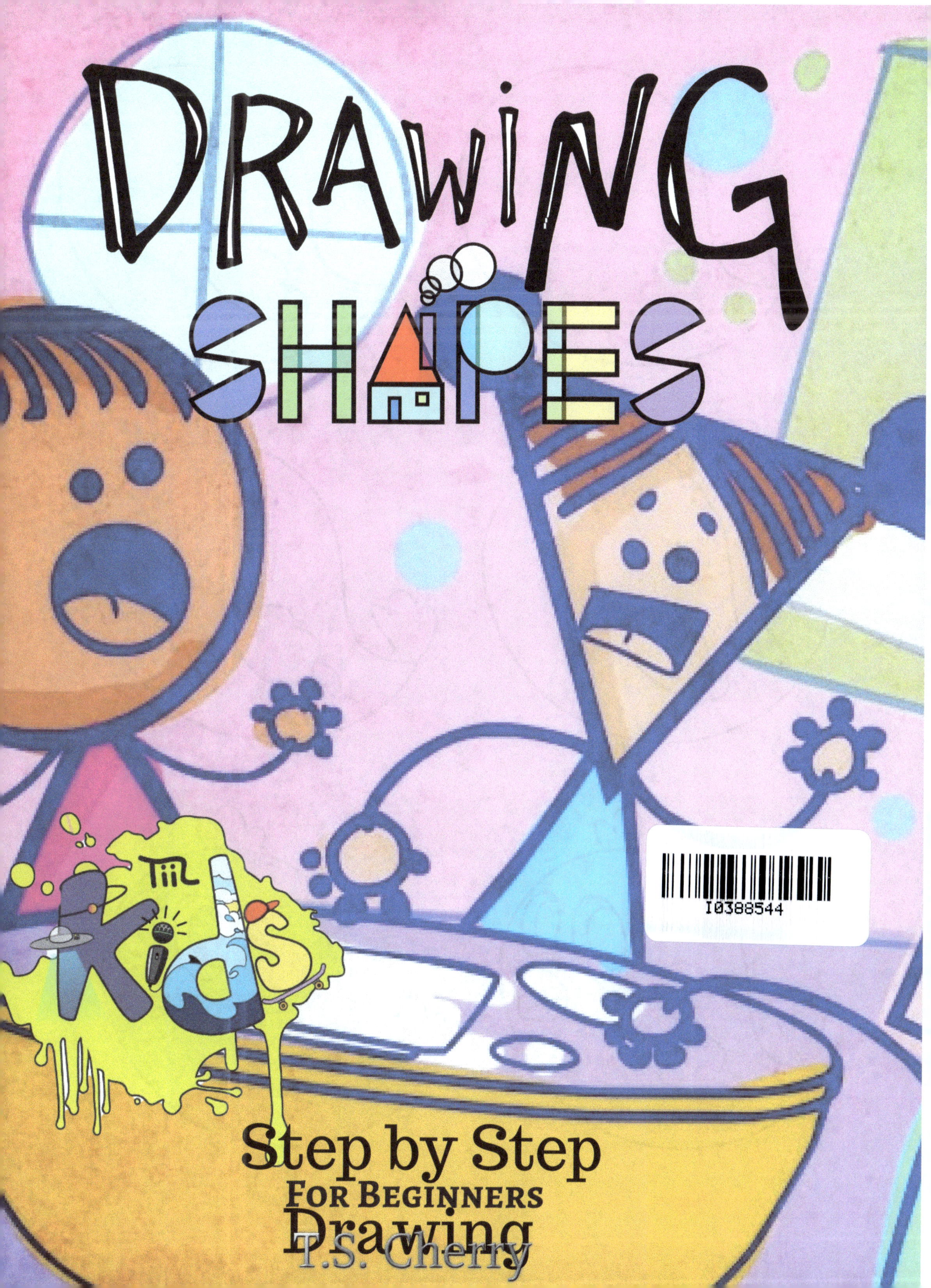

Step by Step
FOR BEGINNERS
Drawing

T.S. Cherry

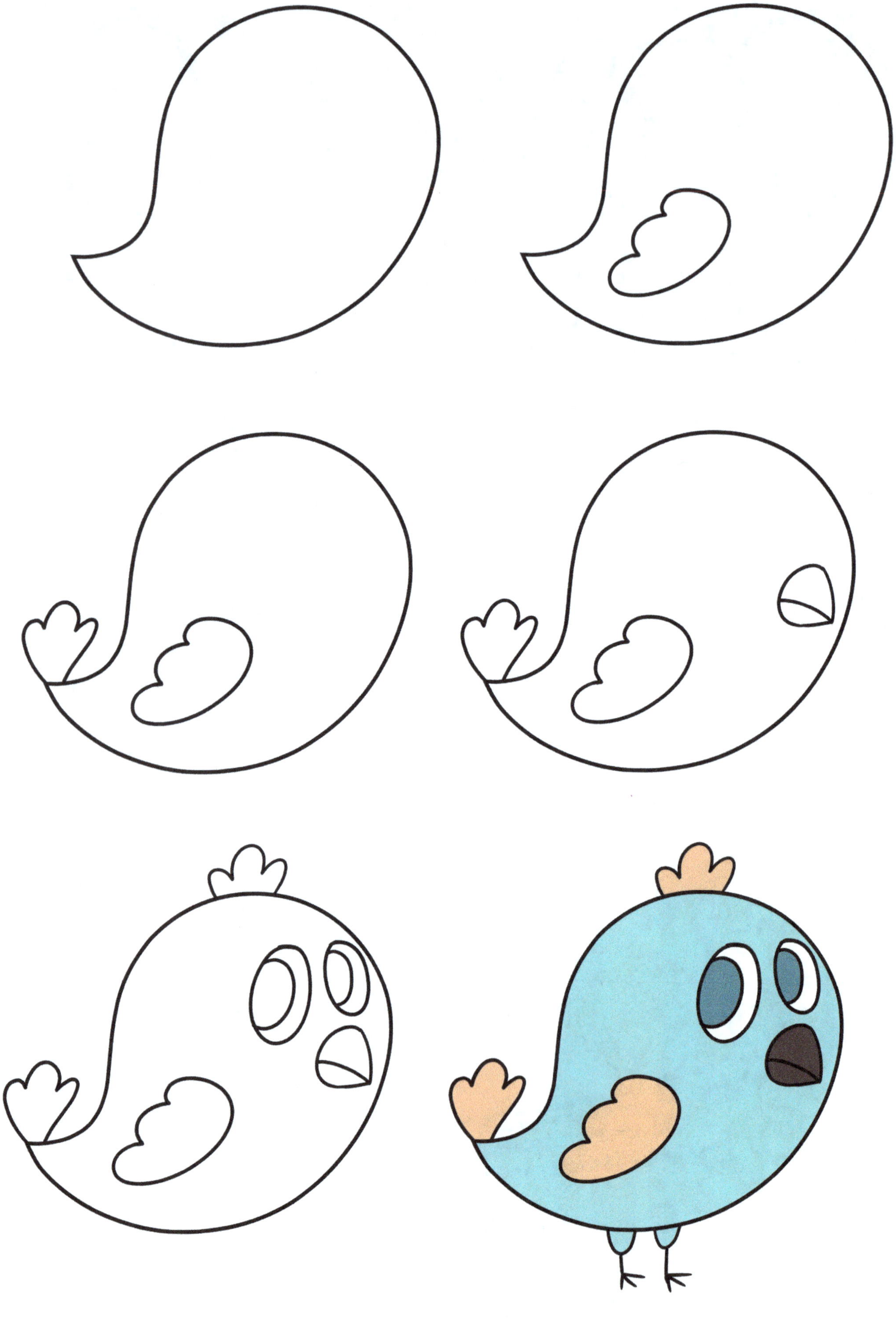

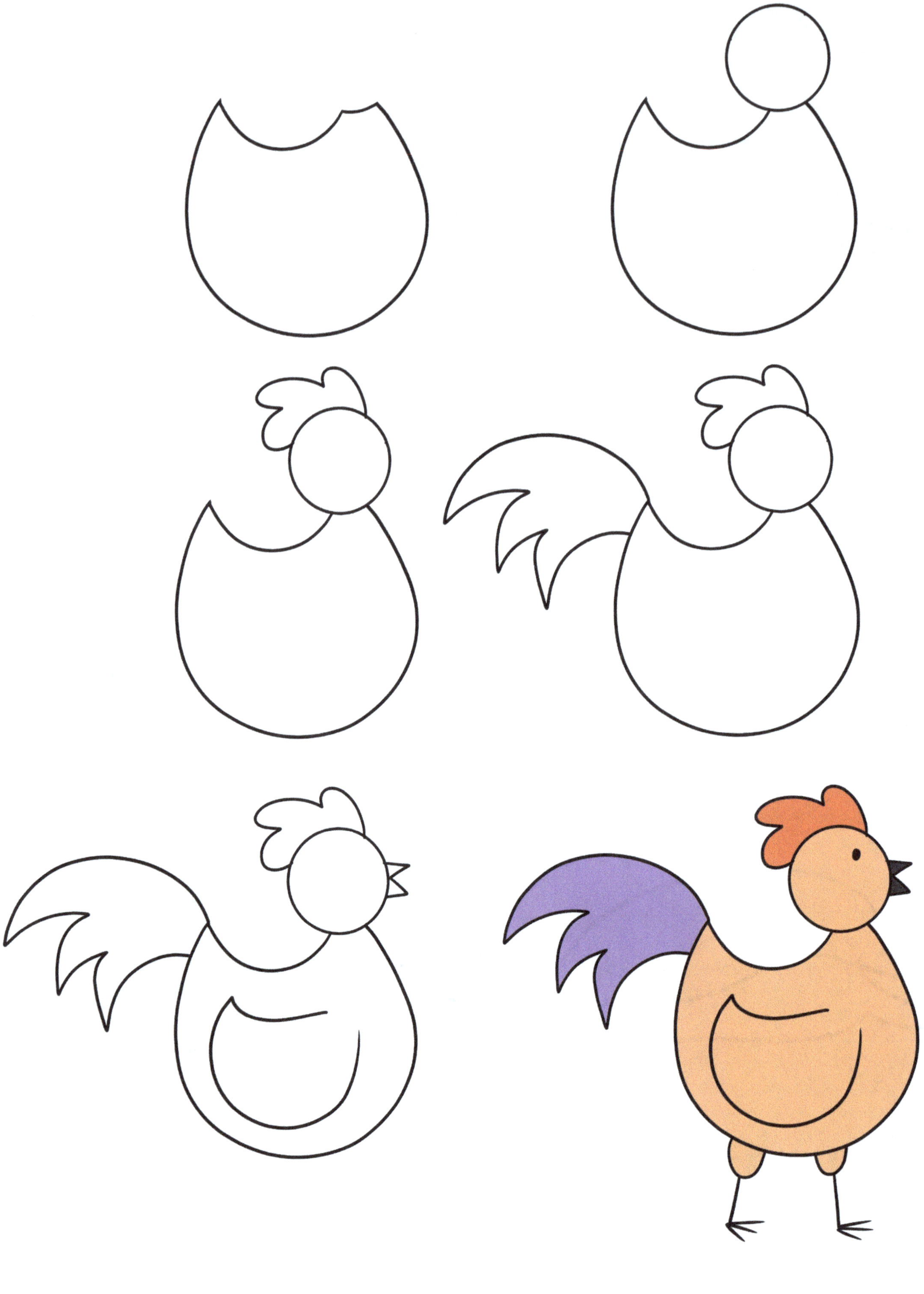

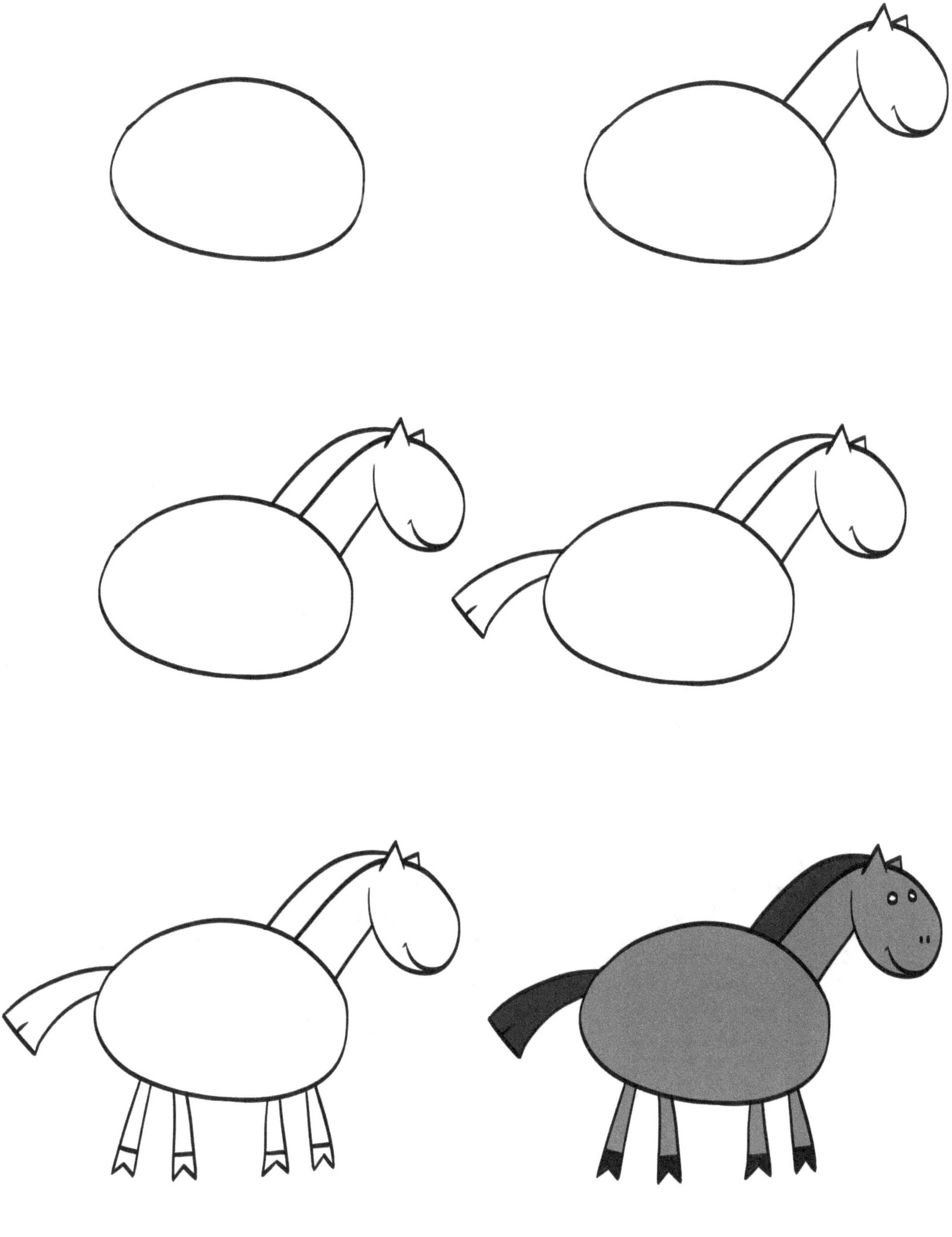

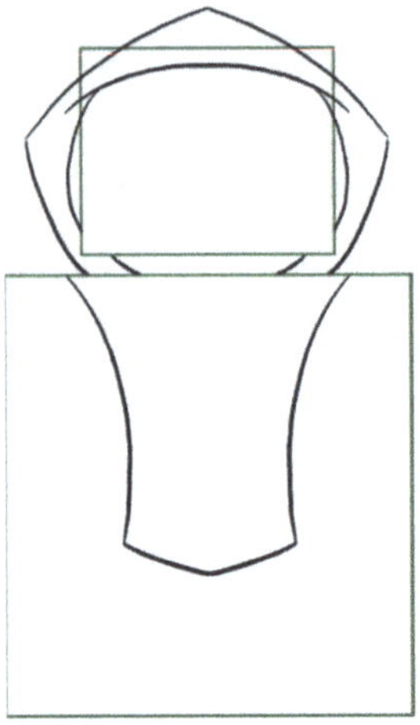

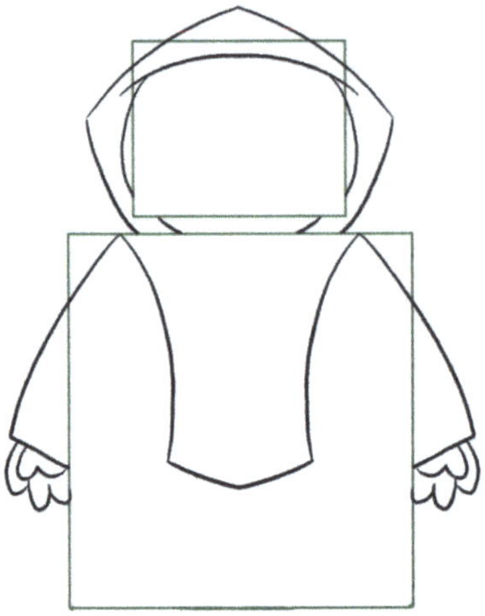

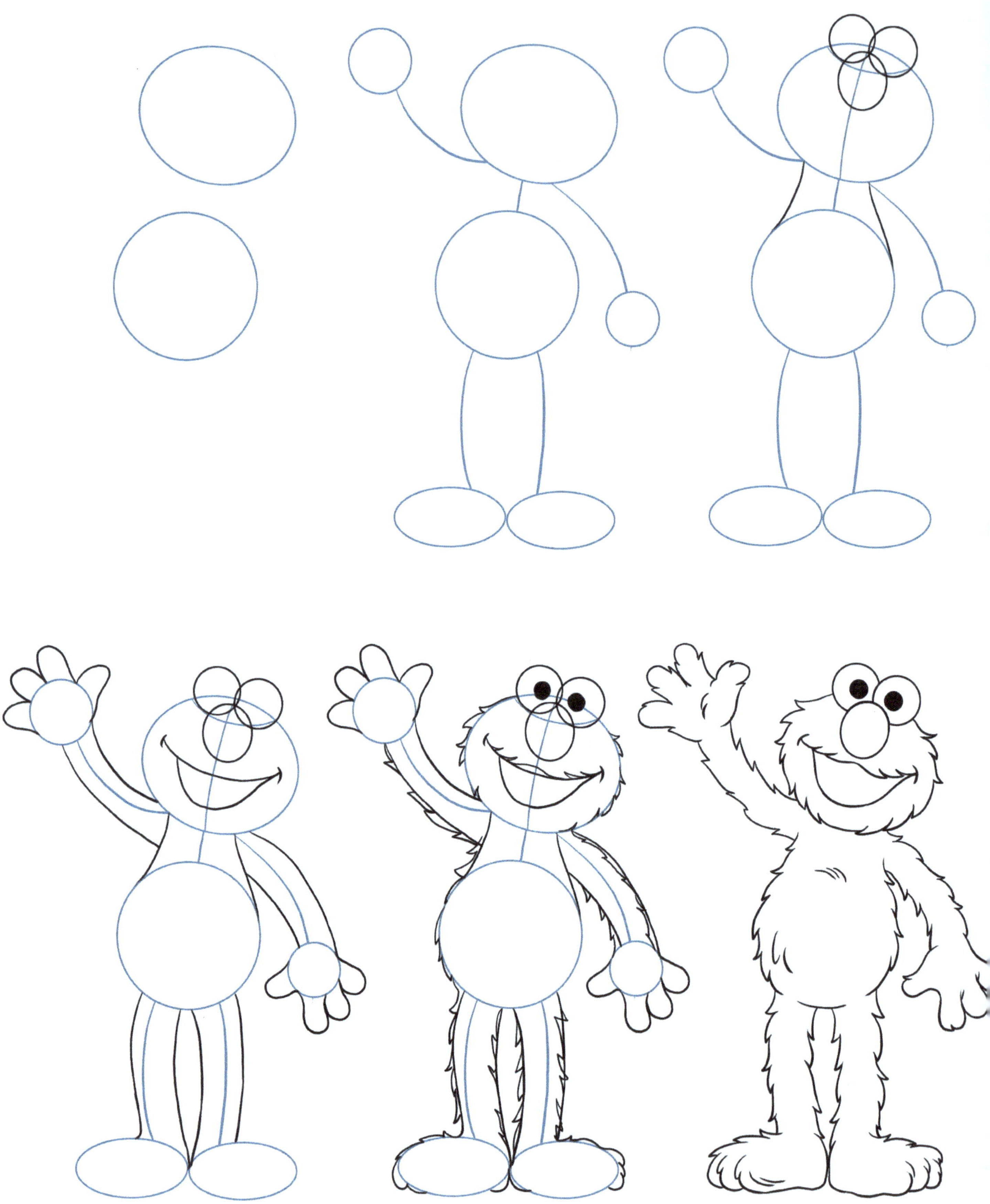

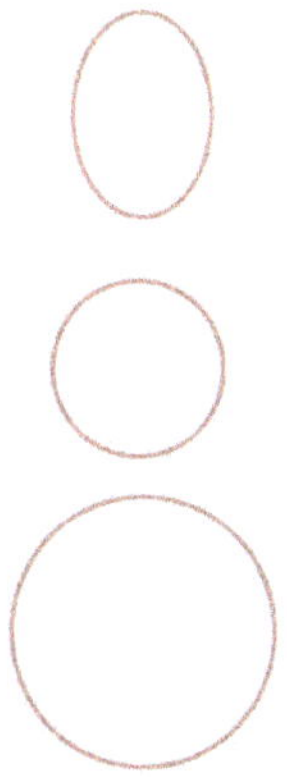

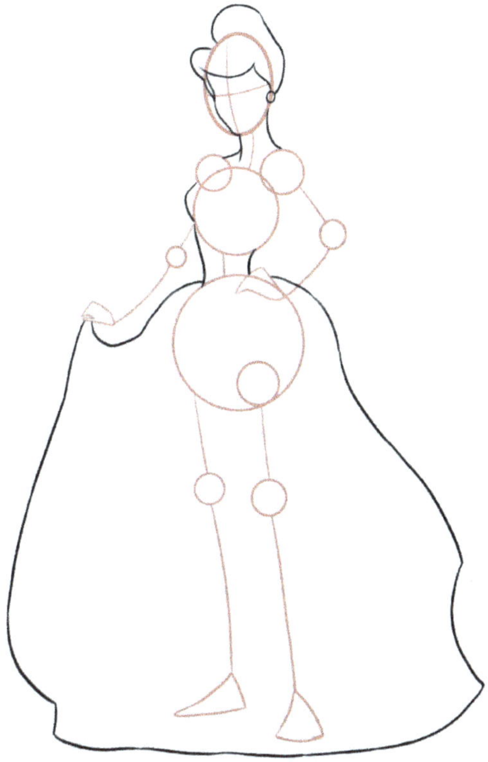

www.ingramcontent.com/pod-product-compliance
Lightning Source LLC
Chambersburg PA
CBHW081358080526
44588CB00016B/2529
* 9 7 8 1 9 4 7 0 2 9 0 9 5 *